In Our Own Write

PRAISE FOR *IN OUR OWN WRITE*

In Our Own Write is a deeply moving, shockingly revealing, funny and
courageously optimistic collection of self-reflective poetry that clearly
illustrates how constructive compassion and the ability to listen, can serve to
not only ease the burden from the marginalized adolescent's shoulders but
more importantly perhaps, show the way to empowerment by helping to
locate their own artistic expression. The importance of the work that Dino
Jacovides and Celyn Jones are doing with inner city teenagers with literacy
issues cannot be overestimated. Just like Unicef's Convention Of The Rights
Of The Child, it focuses on Rights, Respect and Responsibility for its
subject, gives a public voice to a disaffected youth, while building important
bridges between social alienation and mainstream acceptance.
Mark McGann (Artistic Director, Drama Direct)

"The work is extraordinary"
Charles Sturridge, Film Maker

"We should never underestimate the power of poetry and this collection
of poems written by students of Pendragon School is both challenging
and uplifting."
Sir Steve Bullock, Mayor of Lewisham

'The honesty of the children is refreshing and beautiful'
Camila Batmangelijh, Kids Company

This book of extraordinary, poignant, heart warming and heart rending
poetry brought tears to my eyes, both of pleasure and pain. These teenagers
have been given the chance to express their emotions and life experiences in
a way that must, hopefully, be cathartic and life affirming allowing them to
resolve some of the huge challenges they so obviously must have faced and
are still facing. It is a tribute to both Dino Jacovides and Celyn Jones
empathy and compassion that allowed these young adults to express
themselves in a world that so often ignores and marginalizes young people
who do not fit in with the harsh reality of today's society. I applaud them all
for the searing honesty that shines out of all the poems in this wonderful
book *In Our Own Write*.
Caroline Guinness

"Moving, vibrant, packing the ferocious punch of those fully alive."
"In our own write reads like despaches from the urban frontline."
You want to know what it's like to be an inner city teenager in 21st century
britain? This anthology tells you, with wit, purpose and poignancy . The
achievements of these wriers cannot be underestimated, nor the skills and
passion of Artists In Residence, who supplied the fire for this crucible.
An urgent, immediate and powerful read. Highly reccommended.
Kaite O'Reilly - Playwright

In Our Own Write

Poems by students of Pendragon School

Facilitated by Dino Jacovides

Matador
9 De Montfort Mews
Leicester LE1 7FW, UK
Tel: (+44) 116 255 9311 / 9312
Email: books@troubador.co.uk
Web: www.troubador.co.uk/matador

ISBN 1 906221 324

Photographs by Marysia Lachowicz

Typeset in 12pt Bembo by Troubador Publishing Ltd, Leicester, UK

Matador is an imprint of Troubador Publishing Ltd

PREFACE

I am proud and privileged to have played a small part in instigating the development of such an innovative project that has captured an impetus at Pendragon School to further develop creativity across the curriculum.

The stated vision of Pendragon School is 'Anything is Possible'.

This is transmitted to students in a wide range of challenging media-inspired learning experiences which aim to help our students overcome some of their difficulties with language and communication. They are facilitated by the range of in-house artists and their various acting, poetry, artist, photography, film and radio programme making backgrounds and experiences.

In Our Own Write is the culmination of a year's work, designed to show students that their life stories have value and reflects, in some cases, some of the hardships encountered and personal tragedies experienced. The students have shown great interest in being given the opportunity to reflect on their emotions and experiences with Celyn Jones and Dino Jacovides to produce their first published book of poetry. They have also developed a better understanding of the fact that the ability to convey information and thoughts does not solely depend upon the ability to write. This awareness has given them a freedom of expression that, interestingly, has helped them gain confidence and also led them to develop an interest in the written word and their use of it.

Pendragon students are proud of what they have produced. Staff have enjoyed working with and being able to help them.

It has been possible.

Pancho Martinez

PMartin2

Headteacher

INTRODUCTION

Pendragon School gained specialist school status in September 2005 in the subject areas of English, Citizenship and Drama. A central theme of the specialist school plan has been in the development of student voice, providing curriculum opportunities for students to gain confidence and work towards emotional literacy. This project has contributed significantly to this and, in addition, has enhanced the students' literary awareness.

I read many of the poems as they were produced. I have also heard several of them performed, either live or as a recording, by the students themselves. These performances are both moving and extremely powerful. Knowing each of these students well, I recognise the enormous effort they have made in order to produce work of this standard and, in many cases, being very honest about their personal histories, hopes and fears.

Joanna Tarrant
Deputy Headteacher

FOREWORD

In April 2006 I was asked to come and work with students from Pendragon School to help them create pieces of self-reflective poetry. It was initially meant to be a project that lasted a term with a small cluster of students ranging from 13–15 years of age. The project's early success became a whole year's work with twenty-four students, culminating in the publishing of this book, *In Our Own Write*. Having worked extensively over a number of years in various schools, I relished the fresh challenge and all of its presumed obstacles.

The process has been the most enlightening of my eight-year career as a poet in education. The challenges faced by the poor literacy and communication skills of some of the students had to be overcome with unorthodox techniques, in contrast with those that may be used in a mainstream school.

The students weren't very trusting to begin with, and who could blame them? They were being asked to come out of their class and sit for approximately forty-five minutes with a stranger to write poetry. Therefore I began with general familiarisation, just having a chat and finding out what they liked and disliked. An important part of this building process was for me not to be afraid of revealing myself, my likes and dislikes, such as films, music and what football team I support. This proved to be priceless, as it provided a cornerstone for banter, objective argument and, of course, friendship.

The process of writing the poetry came from a lot of lengthy discussions about personal feelings and outlooks; and about how each student saw their own role within society, with me frantically writing down key points and direct quotes along with general information such as '*How many brothers and sisters do you have?*' and '*What's your favourite food?*'. I must reiterate that the literacy skills of each individual were not very high, due to learning difficulties and not a lack of effort; therefore, to maximise our time together and for each student to speak freely, I penned the writing.

The questions I asked would become more involved and complex for the students as time went on, as trust had been built and they felt comfortable enough for me to challenge some of their answers. A key question I would often ask is '*What would you do if you ruled the world?*'

After the usual answers of '*I'd have a mansion and spend loads of money,*' we began to delve into more social problems such as street crime and poverty.

I started structuring their main points on the page in the layout of a poem, allowing the students to be clear about what they had presented. Together we set about adapting and elaborating on their chosen key issues.

What follows is an eclectic mix of work that I and, more importantly, the students are extremely proud of. I hope you enjoy the pieces and appreciate the time and effort spent and the barriers that had to be overcome by each and every one of the writers.

Dino Jacovides – Writer in Residence ltd

"We shall not cease from exploration, and the end of all our exploring will be to arrive where we started and know the place for the first time."
TS Eliot

In November 2004 I arrived at Pendragon School in Downham to deliver a Days Drama workshop, unknown to me we were at the start of a creative odyssey together that would span three years and multiple art forms culminating in the production of the highest quality Drama, Music and Poetry.

It never ceases to inspire when I see the willingness to create with different artists from the students whose bravery and choices are constantly supported by a talented and passionate core of staff led by Pancho Martinez and Joanna Tarrant.

As Artists they've challenged their environments, as young people they've remained positive and open to new ideas leaving all who surround them humbled and moved by nothing more than human honesty; I feel privileged to be one of those.

So here they are with a published anthology of their poetry, just another piece of evidence that amongst a challenging world full of external pressures and distant dreams, Art will find a way and Young people will have their say, "Anything is possible."

Celyn Jones
Actor: Artists in Residence ltd

A MINUTE FROM.....

You don't see me
But I see you
Struggling to understand me
Believing
I don't dream like you do
I don't sleep and breathe
Like you do
I'm alive through and through
As the winter turns to summer
I can feel the heat
And touch the snow
But things don't flow
In the way that you know
I've pushed mountains aside
And inhaled the sun's mighty glow
I keep the wheels turning
On this one-man show
I'm a minute from midnight
At the edge of the world
I struggle in the darkness
Sometimes losing my way
But I'm still the King and Queen
Of all I survey
I scream when I'm hurting
And laugh when it's right
I'm the last glow at sunset
And the first star at night
I'm a minute from midnight
At the edge of the world
The sirens are flashing
I'm blinded by lights

I don't want to be just
Another number
In urban street life
Where blink flash knife
Or
Reverberating gun
Is part of the show
You don't go where I go
Because I'm in the know
Blow out your excuses and listen to me
I've got old man's knowledge
And I'm not yet sixteen
I'm a minute from midnight
At the edge of the world
Will you remember me
When the day is done
The race is run
You've had your fun
Through mistrusting eyes
My guise says I'm happy
As you accuse me of lies
I've never quit a day in my life
My strength stays
With me
I'm "gonna" be
Who
I "wanna" be
One day
You will see me fly
With the smile of a lullaby
I'm a minute from midnight
At the edge of the world.

Dino Jacovides

LOST LIVES

I'm black and I'm proud
I see people come outside your house
To do stuff to you
Them workers
They stamp on your trainers
Them workers
They're afraid
Them workers
Paranoid and scared
They think everyone's out to get them

They try to get me
They expect me
To fight back
But I don't want to get myself hurt

Black on black
It don't make sense
Being from the same area
Same blood
And fighting each other.
People make fun
Because I'm African
But I'm a man
Just like them.

There's fear of the streets
I get paranoid
Every time
I walk
That someone's
Going to jump me

When I go
To meet my friends
In my ends

They try to get me
They expect me
To fight back
But I don't want to get myself hurt

Jumping trains
Music up loud
People telling me to turn it down
They don't like rap music
But music is music
They shouldn't have a problem.

Places are racist
People saying Abraham
Is a camel's name
Even though my name's
From the bible
Ancient and powerful

They try to get me
They expect me
To fight back
But I don't want to get myself hurt

People get pissed when I
Knock on the door
Ask a girl to come out
Brother screams and shouts
Chases me down

But I jump on the bus
A cuss is a cuss
And there's no one to trust

People laugh at me
Because
I stay downstairs
People are racist
'Cos I'm darker than them
I'm smarter than them
I don't know why they're racist
They think it's funny
Because I'm black

They try to get me
They expect me
To fight back
But I don't want to get myself hurt

Mixed race
Don't like my face
How can they even
Let
A
White
Girl
Be racist to me?
Can't they see
That I'm true black

Abraham Lakoni aged 15

WAITING FOR YOU

Where have you been?
Gone for five years
I've been in tears
Waiting for you
You expect everything to be all right
It'll never be the same
It was my mum who had to fight
Whilst you were far away
With the girls on your dream date
15 different girls but never my mum
But I'm nearly 15 now
And you missed your chance
To see me grow
You're looking at me now
But you're getting older by the second.
I reckon
God wants to blow your brains out

BJ Noonan aged 16

I AM

I AM NICE
I AM FUNNY
I AM FRIENDLY
I AM WISE
I AM GREAT COMPANY

I FLY AT SUNRISE ON BUBBLY CLOUDS
UNTIL I REACH MY HEAVEN
FULL OF MELLOW JAZZ
LIKE THE SEA.
FEELING RELAXED AS THE WAVES COME IN

I DON'T LIKE BEING UNTRUTHFUL
I DON'T LIKE BEING RUDE
I DON'T LIKE MY HUMOUR
I DON'T LIKE GETTING TOLD OFF

I WANT TO BE LOVED
I WANT TO BE LIKED
I WANT TO BE GOOD
I WANT TO BE TRUTHFUL
I WANT TO BE BACK IN TOUCH WITH MY DAD

I FLY AT SUNRISE ON BUBBLY CLOUDS
UNTIL I REACH MY HEAVEN
FULL OF MELLOW JAZZ
LIKE THE SEA.
FEELING RELAXED AS THE WAVES COME IN

I DON'T WANT TO BE LET DOWN
I DON'T WANT TO BE CALLED A LIAR
I DON'T WANT TO BE CALLED A LOSER
I DON'T WANT TO BE PICKED ON

I DREAM OF MY NEW NEPHEW BEING BORN
I DREAM OF BEING A SINGER, WHAT MORE!
I DREAM OF MY CAREER AND MY OWN HOME
I DREAM OF BEING REMEMBERED WHEN I'M
GONE

I FLY AT SUNRISE ON BUBBLY CLOUDS
UNTIL I REACH MY HEAVEN
FULL OF MELLOW JAZZ
LIKE THE SEA.
FEELING RELAXED AS THE WAVES COME IN

Kali Perkins aged 15

OPEN FIRE

Army cadets
Cock
Barrel
Gun
Strip it
Clean it
Run ten miles
With orders on your back

Camp at night in teams of four
Rifles move from left to right
I always hit the target
Hunting the enemy by moonlight
War games
Trying not to break and arm or a leg

I love danger;
Trying not to trip up
Or get shot in the head
Dodge the trigger aisles and flare guns
Open fire!
My team runs
Regroups and starts again
Get our man out
Front scope
Back scope
Sight's up to
50
100
200

Eat from rations
Got to stay lean
Mean
And ready
Shut your eyes for 45 seconds
So your sight adjusts to the dark
Be ready for the rules of engagement
If they're shooting too far
Then let it go by
If they get near
Then
Open fire!

A team
Well
Oiled machine
Train me up
To go to the army
If I didn't like it I wouldn't go
Want to make my grandad proud
He fought in World War 2
My auntie was in the army
Make her proud too

I'll be the man in the infantry
Then I'll join the military police
But if
I have to kill
I'll be sad and angry
If it's one on one
Then it's them or me

I'd like to be a corporal
And then a sergeant major
But never a general
I don't want the pressure of leading men into war
I don't want the pressure of getting men killed
I want to join to help people
Who can't help themselves
To stop corruption in terrible places

Mitchell Sillick aged 14

TRUTH IS......

I don't like being bossed around
Makes me feel angry
And sometimes I cry.

I've only got one pair of hands
YOU KNOW!
Don't boss me around
I end up feeling like a slave!

Truth is
I'm a liar
I lie a lot
And blame others
I wish I didn't because
I get into trouble
As I always get caught
I steal cakes and biscuits
From inside the house
And then I lie!

I don't want to
But I can't help it
I try to stop
But it doesn't work
I lie about time
When I watch TV over an hour
When really
I should be
Having a shower.

And then......
We argue

And I get upset
Just because I forget
To turn off
The television set.

Sometimes I'm accused
When I didn't even lie
And blame it on
One of my invisible friends
Because I can see him
And you can't
'Joey Weeler,'
That's who I blame.

He causes a lot of trouble
To my other invisible friends.
I have trouble asking for things
It's very difficult for me
So I just take.

Sometimes I get away with it
And sometimes I don't.
Sometimes I do it
To annoy others
For shouting at me
When they shouldn't tell me **WHAT TO DO!**
They should just let me be
I don't lie in school though
Because I like it here

Donna Muerto aged 14

MANNERS

Sometimes I think life is a dream
That I've died before and come back
I look to the sky
Because when I was poor
Seems like a life before
God saved me so I can see tomorrow
The day before
When I'm asleep
I can see the future
During the day
I dream at night
That I am dead
Someone shot me
And I'm covered in sweat
I don't want to die
When I wake up
I don't believe that I'm alive

Manners to show
Manners to whatever you do
Manners for life

I was poor in Portugal
My family was poor
When I was born
I lived with my dad
People thought
I'd didn't know how to read
People thought
I never went to school
When I was young
My dad didn't have

A lot of money
To buy me trainers
People cuss me and call me names

When I was a young boy
I believed in God
And God helped me
Get a good family
And I left Portugal

Manners to show
Manners to whatever you do
Manners for life

People used to beat me and say:
'You have nothing!'
They see me now
Strong and with money
When I go back I'm proud
Now they're jealous
And that makes me feel good
A long time ago people thought I'd
Never leave the country
But I went to Brazil with my dad.
My dad's worked hard
And he's not poor anymore
I had enough in Portugal
And thought;
'That life's got to change'

Manners to show
Manners to whatever you do

Manners for life

One day
People will see me
Wearing an Arsenal shirt
Number 13
Burning down the wing
And then I will be on top of the world.

I live in Brixton
And some times I've got to fight
To shut people up
I turn into the devil
When they want to play rough
When really
All I want to do
Is help my family

Manners to show
Manners to whatever you do
Manners for life

Raphael Figuerido (16)

PIE!

I DON'T LIKE PEOPLE
BEING HORRIBLE TO ME
MAKES ME SAD AND ANGRY
I GET ANNOYED
WHEN I
HAVE TO GO TO MY ROOM
WHEN I'M
NAUGHTY

OH AND I DON'T LIKE PIE!

I LIVE IN THE TOP HALF OF THE
HOUSE
WITH MY MUM AND DAD
I WISH WE HAD
THE WHOLE
HOUSE
SO I COULD
GO UP
AND DOWN
I'D LIKE TO
MOVE
DOWNSTAIRS
AND THEN
COME BACK UP

OH AND I DON'T LIKE PIE!

I LIKE PLAYING IN MY BEDROOM
I LIKE PLAYING WITH SHENEZE
I LIKE PLAYING IN THE GARDEN
I LIKE EASTENDERS

BUT OH I DON'T LIKE PIE!

MY FAVOURITE COLOUR IS RED
MY FAVOURITE DRINK IS FANTA
I'M NICE
KIND
HAPPY
AND SMILEY

OH I LOVE SHEPHERD'S PIE AND CHIPS!

Katy Silva aged 14

HAPPY LIFE

I WANT A HAPPY LIFE
I WANT TO BE BY MYSELF
NO-ONE TELLING ME WHAT TO DO
I DON'T WANT TONY- BUSH

I WANT SOLAR-POWERED CARS
THAT DON'T PUKE POLLUTION
NO MORE AEROPLANES
NO GREEN HOUSE EFFECTS

I WANT TO BE FRIENDLY TO THE
ENVIRONMENT

HOWEVER
MY SPECIALITY
IS GETTING ON PEOPLE'S NERVES
TO GET ATTENTION
OR DETENTION

I'D RATHER TURN THE WORLD BLACK
THAN HAVE THIEVES
BREAKING IN
STEALING
THINGS FROM OUR HOUSES
FROM OUR LIVES
LET'S STOP THE STABBING WITH THEIR KNIVES
I'D RATHER THERE'D BE NO LIGHT
ALL BLACK
SO THEY CAN'T SEE US
AND STOP THEIR ATTACK

I WANT TO GO TO BRAZIL
AND BE FREE
IN THE AMAZON
OR THE ANDES
NO-ONE CHASING ME
I'D TAKE MY MUM WITH ME
'COS SHE'S SPECIAL TO ME

I WANT TO HIDE FROM THE WORLD
CRIME
GUN SHOTS
STABBINGS
PICK POCKETING
I'D RATHER BE WITH ANIMALS
THAN PEOPLE
AT LEAST
THEY'RE HONEST
AT LEAST
THEY LEAVE YOU ALONE
I WANT A HAPPY LIFE
I WANT TO BE BY MYSELF.

Daniel Barton aged 15

I LIVE IN NEW CROSS

I'm cocky!

I don't like dogs
Bad teenagers should
Get punished
Make them live alone
I'm not scared anymore
I've learnt to stand up for myself
Too much violence in the world

I'm Funny!

My dream is to be an actor,
Footballer for Arsenal
Or an athlete

Mature sometimes!

If I ruled the world
I'd stop the suffering everywhere
Give poor people money
Instead of the government
Taking it all
I'd give schools healthy food
The food is unhealthy
It annoys me
Everybody's equal
We all bleed red
Too much violence in the world

Violent sometimes!

It's sickening
That the
Littering has gone too far
Chicken and chips on the floor
It's disgusting
If you don't want it
Bin it
There's rats on the street
They come and eat everything that you leave

Confident!

I dream to live alone
Where no-one can tell me what to do
Somewhere without neighbours
Who make too much noise
Too much violence in the world

Calm......

Patrick Elue aged 13

I CARE

I CARE ABOUT MY FAMILY
BECAUSE THEY'VE BEEN THERE SINCE I WAS
BORN
I CARE ABOUT MY FRIENDS
BECAUSE THEY MAKE ME LAUGH
I CARE ABOUT THE WORLD
AND WANT TO HELP THE POOR
I WANT TO HELP THE STARVING
I WANT TO HELP THEM ALL
I WANT TO HELP CURE CANCER
AND TERRIBLE DISEASE

I WANT TO GET RID OF MURDER
I WANT TO GET RID OF RAPE
IT WOULD MAKE THE WORLD HAPPY
AND IT'LL BE A SAFER PLACE
I WANT TO LIVE IN LINCOLNSHIRE
AT MY AUNTIE'S HOUSE
LOOKING AFTER HER CHILDREN
AND PICKING LOVELY FLOWERS

I WANT TO BE A SINGER
AND FAMOUS ON THE STAGE
I WANT PEOPLE TO KNOW ME
AND I'D BE FRIENDS WITH ALL THE STARS

I CARE ABOUT WHAT PEOPLE THINK
DON'T WANT THEM TO THINK I'M BAD
I'M REALLY
REALLY
REALLY
NICE
MY NAME'S RACHEL AND I AM GLAD

Rachel Tierny aged 15

ALBANIA

I come from Albania
I don't want war
No wars
No slavery.

What I want
Is peace
The kind of peace
I want is
To be
Kind
Helping the poor
Don't want to see death anymore
I want to help
My brother
My father
My mother
My family and friends

I'm tired of getting angry
And having to fight
On the bus
Because people don't like my music

I'm Albanian
And proud of it
So I turn it up loud
Why should I turn my music off?

In an ideal world
We'd all live how we want
Happy

And
Free
Talking to girls
With blonde golden hair
With eyes as blue as the sea
This makes me smile
When they're looking at me

Sometime I don't wanna come to school
I wake up and my head's hammering
Brain battering
I'm lazy
Unless on the street
Where
There's
Cameras looking at me
But they don't always catch me
Can't jam without getting
Into a fight
Police stop me
And ask
For name and details
But I don't want to fight all my life
But if people start
Then I've got no choice
Time to go to a new school
I don't like it here
It embarrasses me
I lie about coming here
So no-one knows
Except my family

Hazret Sokoli aged 14

CIGARETTES and CHAINS

I SHOW A FRONT
SO PEOPLE DON'T TAKE ADVANTAGE
LOOK TOUGH ON THE OUTSIDE
SO PEOPLE DON'T ASK ME TO DO STUFF
FOR THEM
LIKE BUY
CIGARETTES
CHAINS
EARRINGS
ALCOHOL
I'D RATHER DO IT TO THEM INSTEAD
SO THEY THINK THAT I'M BAD AND VIOLENT
SO THEY DON'T COME NEAR ME
THEY FEAR ME
ALTHOUGH THIS UPSETS ME
I DO IT ANYWAY
IT'LL BE BETTER IF I COULD TRUST THEM
BUT
IT DON'T WORK LIKE THAT

MAYBE ONE DAY
THINGS WILL CHANGE
MAYBE ONE DAY
PEOPLE WON'T BE SCARED OF ME
THEY'LL BE MY FRIENDS INSTEAD

FEEL LIKE I HAVE TO FIGHT
SO PEOPLE DON'T THINK I'M WEAK
THERE'S NO OTHER WAY
I WISH THERE WAS
BUT LIFE AIN'T THAT WAY
IT'S HARD

IT'S TOUGH
IT'S DANGEROUS
FEEL LIKE I HAVE TO PROTECT MY FRIENDS

MAYBE ONE DAY
THINGS WILL CHANGE
MAYBE ONE DAY
PEOPLE WON'T BE SCARED OF ME
THEY'LL BE MY FRIENDS INSTEAD

ONE DAY I WANT A FAMILY
AND A HUSBAND
I WANT TO BE A FOOTBALLER'S WIFE
LIVING THE GLAMOUR LIFE
FAMOUS AND WANTED
THEN MY BROTHERS CAN LIVE WITH ME
AND SIT BY THE POOL
DRINKING BACARDI BREEZERS
EATING CHOCOLATE
AND PLAYING AROUND
LETTING MY FAMILY JAM FOR FREE

MAYBE ONE DAY
THINGS WILL CHANGE
MAYBE ONE DAY
PEOPLE WON'T BE SCARED OF ME
THEY'LL BE MY FRIENDS INSTEAD

Vanessa Osboune aged 15

MASH AND LIQUER

Favourite food?
'I EAT ANYTHING
DON'T LIKE VEGTABLES!
LOVE PIE
MASH AND LIQUER'

What else do you like James?
'I LIKE JOKES
A STEAK AND KIDNEY PIE WALKS INTO A PUB
AND ASKS FOR A PINT
BAR MAN SAYS,
SORRY MATE WE DON'T SERVE HOT FOOD'

'I LIKE DETECTIVE PROGRAMMES
WHEN EATING
SAUSAGE AND CHIPS.
MORSE
AND FROST
MAKE ME LAUGH AND MAKE ME THINK.'

How was the holiday James?
'WHEN IS A DOOR NOT A DOOR?'
I don't know. When?
'WHEN IT'S A JAR'

'STATIC CARAVAN CLOSED IN WINTER
IT'LL BE OPEN SOON
HOME FROM HOME
I'VE GOT A FRIEND
WHO'S SOMETIMES THERE.
MY NAN AND GRANDDAD
ARE THINKING OF MOVING SO THEY'RE ALWAYS

IN KENT
IT'S FRIENDLIER DOWN THERE
IF YOU SAY 'GOOD MORNING'
PEOPLE SAY IT BACK
BUT THEY DON'T AT HOME.'

How would you change the world James?
'I WANT TO FEED THE STARVING
TRY AND STOP ALL THE WARS
I DON'T WANT THEM TO HAPPEN ANYMORE
I LOVE THE PEACE AND QUIET
IN MY STATIC CARAVAN.

I DON'T LIKE PEOPLE CUSSING
HAVE THEY GOT NOTHING BETTER TO DO?'

What else James?
'TWO COLDS WALK INTO A BAR
ONE SAYS TO THE OTHER
COME ON MATE COUGH UP'

Where do you like going?
'DOWN TO THE PUB FOR DINNER
BUT IF MUM'S YAPPING
ABOUT SHOPPING
THEN I GO SIT IN THE CAR
LISTEN TO MUSIC
ON
MY WALKMAN'

Do you like the journey down to the caravan site?
'THERE WAS A TIME ON
THE WAY THERE
WHEN I NEARLY FELL ASLEEP

BUT CHAZ AND DAVE
WERE PLAYING
SO I
SOON WOKE UP.'

James Allen aged 15

RED

Sometimes I erupt like a volcano
When I get angry
Friends make me angry when they say things I don't like

I don't like drunk people
Because they're loud on a Saturday night
Opening the door on moving buses and jumping off
People get violent
Sometimes killing others
That's sad
They're sad when they wake up
They should tell the police
Do the right thing
But do they?

I don't like Forest Hill
It's violent
Not safe at night
Not quiet where I live
Noises give me a headache
Police don't come to our area
Once they came
Handcuffed a man called Jack
Pushed him against the car
He was trying to fight his way out
Arguing
Don't like arguing with my mum
She makes me argue

Everyone should clean up the street
Streets need to be clean so
We can be healthier
And the environment could be cleaner
Build homes for poor and elderly
In the millennium dome
Turn the space into flats
Making the world a safer place
Steven McAuley (14)

HELP EVERYWHERE IN THE WORLD

Help animals that have been mistreated
Neglected
Help the children and the elderly
With
Everyday things
Food
Clothes
And water

Help everywhere in the world
So we can live in peace

Give people what they need
Keep them healthy
Stop the wars
So innocent people don't have to die
Children and parents don't have to cry

Help everywhere in the world
So we can live in peace

I want to leave Brockley
There's a whole world out there
Maybe I can help stop the violence
Too many police sirens
As soon as you hit the city
The sirens hit you back

Help everywhere in the world
So we can live in peace

Out of the city everyone is calm
Relaxed

Nobody rushing about too much
Taking their time
No rush hour
Just blue skies and green grass
The world is ok and could be a lot of fun
If we work hard and earn an honest living
We have to be honest with one another
We have to get rid of robberies and murdering violence
Live together and enjoy ourselves
Help everywhere in the world
So we can live in peace

We need more parks so people can play
And breathe fresh air during the day
It's the only place to go that's safe
Can't play outside
Because
Some people are violent
Doing drugs.

Even though
It's their choice
With
What
They do with their lives
I'd rather people didn't come up to us
Asking for money
When we're in the car
They say they need it for their children
But really
They're just buying drugs
These people are stupid
They think they're clever
But they get addicted
And they're stuck forever

Help everywhere in the world
So we can live in peace

Should be more police
They only come to the area occasionally
There's violence
At night sometimes
Police in the street with cameras
Look for a criminal
Everything happens at once
Scary
Hour
Before they sort it out
Block the road so the person they're chasing
Cannot get out
I'm kind of used to it
But doesn't mean I like it

Help everywhere in the world
So we can live in peace

I'd like to go to Australia or Spain
Nice and hot
It's peaceful and the sun makes
Everyone happy
People could be happier over here
If it was sunny and hot
Because there's more to do
I'd like to go to the London eye
Nice view!

Help everywhere in the world
So we can live in peace

Gemma Leigh aged 15

CHANGE THE EARTH

Change the earth
Give it brighter flowers
They're not bright enough
People would love the flowers
And be better for it
Happier
They'd stop bad things like mugging
Rapes
Abuse and murder
No one would call you names and take things from you
Change the earth
Create new things for autistic people to do
So they can enjoy themselves
Teach them to ride a bike
Like my bike
Change the earth
Change the environment
Because some people don't give a damn
They don't take it into their own hands
Too much litter on the streets
Clean it up!
Change the earth
Help the starving
I want to take them all to
A supermarket
Change the earth
I like Grove Park
But when it's dark
People get stabbed and run over
This makes me sad.
Take me to Africa
To play football with my best friend

To live in a cottage and work
Cutting the crop
And the sugar cane
So when people remember my name
They'll think
Of
Kind
Generous
Helpful and willing

Harry Griggs aged 15

MY LIFE

MY LIFE IS FULL OF HAPPINESS
MY LIFE IS FUN
MY LIFE IS FULL OF LOVE
MY LIFE IS AS BRIGHT AS THE SUN

I DON'T WANT BULLIES
I DON'T WANT PEOPLE INTERFERING
I DON'T WANT POVERTY

MY DREAM IS TO GO ON HOLIDAY
MY DREAM IS TO GET A JOB
MY DREAM IS TO GET MARRIED
MY DREAM IS TO GET MY OWN HOME

IN MY WORLD I'D HAVE A MANSION
IN MY WORLD I'D HAVE A GIRLFRIEND
IN MY WORLD I'D BE PRIME MINISTER

Michael Heath aged 15

GANG LIFE

Older
Younger
Run the risk of fights
Sometimes seems like
I got no choice
Don't want to fight
Too many weapons
Old fashioned
Fist to fist

Too many
Guns
Too many knives
Too many shootings
Taking people's lives
Prime Minister
Should be
On the streets
Got to do something
Stop
The kids

Police search
Me
For no reason
Racism can be a problem
Coming from a party
They cuffed me
Trust me
I don't know what to do
Don't want to go to prison
I want to be something in life
But they piss me off

Searching me
Looking for a knife

I live in
Pepyz estate
Deptford
Ghetto

If people don't know you
Then you get moved to
If they know your face
In my ends you'll be safe
If you're coming to get me
My older will protect me
Got no choice
Need to be a younger
Or else I'm alone
Don't know if I like it

Blue borough
Black borough
Rough
I've had enough

Gang life not for me
Too many crazy minds
Too many hustlers
And P.I.M.P.s
At night
There's too many
Fights
I want to be something in life
Gang life not for me.

Chris Lodge aged 14

WHAT I WANT.......

Half English
Half Scottish
I don't like bullies
I don't like
People calling me names
And
I don't like to fight.

This city
Should be a safer place
For kids
Because
People who take drugs
Give it to innocent people
This city needs more police.

Criminals need help
To sort out their lives
There's a woman
Who
Takes drugs on the estate
She's crazy
She needs help
But she'll probably end up in jail.

This is bad because she's got
A little girl
Who
Now lives with her auntie.

Half English
Half Scottish
I don't like bullies
I don't like
People calling me names
And
I don't like to fight.

I like Sydenham
Except
For people
Who
Smoke weed.

When I go into the block
I can smell it
I don't like it
Kids are too violent
I don't like it
Too much fighting and people
Get stabbed
I don't like it
One kid cut another along his face

I want a peaceful
Quiet world
Not loud, loud
With violence
I like people
Who
Work
It's important to earn money.

Half English
Half Scottish
I don't like bullies
I don't like
People calling me names
And
I don't like to fight.

Alfie Hume aged 14

I FEEL

I FEEL UPSET
EVEN THOUGH I DIDN'T KNOW YOU
HADN'T SEEN YOU FOR ELEVEN YEARS
MAYBE I WAS TOO YOUNG
IT WAS TOO EARLY FOR YOU TO GO
NO-ONE TOLD YOU I WAS IN CARE
YOU SHOULD HAVE KNOWN THE TRUTH
I DON'T KNOW A LOT ABOUT YOU
BUT I DO KNOW YOU SAT
IN THE SAME CORNER
OF THE PUB
FOR
19 YEARS
YOU WERE THERE BEFORE I WAS BORN

THANK YOU FOR THE GAELIC RING
YOU GAVE ME JUST BEFORE
YOU PARTED
TAKING ME BACK TO MY
IRISH ROOTS

I SHOULD HAVE SEEN YOU MORE
BUT I DIDN'T GET THE CHANCE
FEELING SAD
I'M ANGRY AND MAD
BECAUSE
YOU DESERVED LONGER THAN 60 YEARS
I'LL CRY 60 TEARS IN YOUR MEMORY

I DON'T REMEMBER YOU FROM BEFORE
BUT I'LL REMEMBER YOU FROM NOW
YOU WERE ALWAYS NICE AND GOOD TO ME
I'LL ALWAYS REMEMBER YOUR SLEEPING FACE
I HOPE YOU'VE GONE TO
A PEACEFUL PLACE
BETTER PLACE
WE'LL ALWAYS REMEMBER YOUR YOUNGER
DAYS.

BJ Noonan aged 15

EVERYONE LIKES CHICKEN AND CHIPS

Live with mum and dad in New Cross
Got two sisters and three brothers
All have children
My 2nd-eldest bro
Is inside for beating someone
Should be out next year

Don't like school
Because
I wake up
Think I'm going to have a nice day
But people wind me up
Ruining it
Can't stand it when people moan
People winding me up
Make me angry
People talking behind my back annoys me
Too much lip around here
I like New Cross
But I've lived there all my life
Want a change
But not sure where to go
I want to
Become a police officer
Stop crime
Stop bullying
Stop all the wars
None of the wars should happen
Every country should be equal
Fair is fair when you lose everything
When war happens it's like someone
Taking your pencil

So you start a fight
When
You
Should

Just get another
Time to protect my country
Too much
Crime
Too much stealing
Too much killing
Need to build more prisons
Murder should be for life
But sometimes
People should be given a second chance
It's hard to know how to solve it.

Ten years from now
I want to be a driver for the police
I want a big house
With a big Land Rover
Married and happy
With my wife.

This world is cool
But it needs more activities for people
To be happy
Like Disney land
People are too bored
So that's why they hang out
On streets and buses.
There will always be fights
People are aggro
There is a reason;

I know there's a reason
Like a million reasons for stress:
Coming home from school
Or having a bad day at work
But people who live near the sea
Are relaxed
Nice sea air
Chills them out.
I'd like to live near the sea
Fresh air
Arcades
Fair rides
And smiles
There's nothing to do around these areas
If you want to do something
You have to jump on a bus and go into the city
If I could start this place again
I would build new houses for people to live in
New schools for a better education
Some teachers are good
Some teachers are bad
Some of the teachers drive students mad
I don't like the rules of school
But we've all got to learn.

I lose my temper too easily
Violence doesn't solve anything
But sometimes I can't help it
If a boy tries to get near my girlfriend
I lash out!
I'm over-protective
Of her
No one touches my girlfriend

I want to be tough so I go to the army cadets
I play rugby
So if you try to mug me
I get angry
And I'll rough you up
I'm always getting bruised
So all I know is
That
Everyone
Loves chicken and chips.

William Wallace aged 15

PEPYZ

*allow – in this poem means stop, disallow

My life
Is bad
Because I always
Have problems
I don't like Lewisham
It's different
It's difficult
Don't like the borough
It stresses me out.
The people ain't friendly
You need to have street cred
To be their friend.

Hustlers
Money makers
Fakers
These days
They're shooting people
Gun crime
I'm scared of being robbed
Stabbed
Shanked

Don't hear sirens
In my estate
We have a community.
Not like
Peypz estate!
They will kill you after
Midnight
People hiding in their flats

Away from the police
With gate doors
So they don't
Get terrorised
Police there a lot
199 bus becomes 999
On Pepyz estate
By mistake.

Some boy said,
'Do you live around here?'

I said 'yes'
And then
Began to run
Pepyz estate is a deli estate
Get gadged
Get jacked
I'm just happy
I live in a community
Nothing bad happens to me
If I lived on Pepyz estate
I'd be dead by now.

Community estate
Is where I live
In
Peabody trust
Deptford
Deptford is bad
'Cos Pepyz is mad
They're everywhere.

Chasing you
To rob you
To kill you

I want a gun if necessary
Shoot my enemies
They deserve it;
For what they've done to me
Threatening me
With a knife
I'll shoot them
If I could
I want them to die
For what they do
Too much killing
Like Damilola Taylor
Clean these streets.

If I was mafia
I'd bring them all to justice
Kill my enemies
Kill that boy with the hat
Who robbed my doughnuts

Violence on violence
'Allow gun crime
'Allow the knives
'Allow the killing

How would you feel if you got stabbed?
Be like suffocation
Under water
Bleed to death
That's it

Your soul is gone.

I'm too fast!
When a boy wants to gadge
Me
In Deptford.
Enough is enough!

I want things back to normal
Back to ghetto fashion
Listening to music
Without any trouble
People are here to make a living
But
People try to rob you
Of your clothes
Leave you
Naked in the street.
I hate it when people look
At me

Some man looked at me on the DLR
Angers me
He carried on staring
What does he want?
I want him to stop
I want it all to stop!

Abraham Lakoni aged 15

I'M NOT A BULLY!

DON'T TALK ABOUT ME
DON'T CUSS ME
DON'T CUSS MY MUM

I'M NOT A BULLY
I JUST HIT PEOPLE
'COS THEY WIND ME UP
I BULLY TO DEFEND MYSELF
SO PEOPLE DON'T THINK I'M WEAK
IF PEOPLE TRY IT
I KNOCK THEM OUT
AND MAKE THEM MY YOUNGER

DON'T TALK ABOUT ME
DON'T CUSS ME
DON'T CUSS MY MUM

MY BROTHER IS RUDE
AND HE LOVES TO FIGHT
NAUGHTY LITTLE MAN
HE GETS INTO TROUBLE

SOMETIMES I WORK
IN CAMBRIDGE
IN THE CAR WASH
I LIKE IT
DRYING THE CARS
WHEN THEY'RE CLEAN

DON'T TALK ABOUT ME
DON'T CUSS ME
DON'T CUSS MY MUM

IN MY ENDS
GIRLS GO TO THE PARK
TO GET DRUNK
IN THE SUMMER.

IN MY ENDS
THERE
ARE A LOT
OF ROBBERIES.
I DON'T SMOKE WEED
OR CIGARETTES

I WISH I WAS INVISIBLE
SO NO-ONE COULD SEE ME
I'D HAUNT THE PEOPLE
THAT ARE BAD TO ME
SCARE THEM
AND GET MY REVENGE

DON'T TALK ABOUT ME
DON'T CUSS ME
DON'T CUSS MY MUM

Hazret Sokoli aged 14

NO!

I'M FIGHTING FOR JUSTICE
PEOPLE TO SEE ME
TO KNOW ME
I'M NOT INTO POLITICS
BUT THE RIGHT TO SAY MY MIND
LIFE'S NOT EASY
BUT THEY SHOULDN'T BE IN IRAQ
WHERE
EVERYDAY IS WORSE THAN BEFORE

NO BLAIR
NO BUSH
NO QUEEN

YOUNG GIRLS HAVE NO DIGNITY ABOUT THEM-
SELVES
THEY'VE LOST SELF RESPECT
YOUNG GIRLS GO AROUND AND WILD
GOVERNMENTS DON'T CARE ABOUT THE
YOUTH OF THEIR COUNTRY
TOO BUSY TAKING OTHER COUNTRIES
INSTEAD OF TAKING CARE OF THEIR YOUTH
SOME BOY GOT SHOT
TWO BOYS GOT SHOT
13 AND 15
WHERE WAS THE GOVERNMENT ON THAT
ESTATE

NO BLAIR
NO BUSH
NO QUEEN

WHEN I CAME TO THIS COUNTRY
I NEEDED HELP
THE SCHOOL DID NOTHING
SENT ME TO ANOTHER SCHOOL
AND ANOTHER SCHOOL
THEY KICKED ME OUT
MUM WROTE TO BLAIR
TO HELP ME OUT
HE WROTE BACK SAYING TO LOOK AGAIN
MUM GOT MAD AND WROTE TO THE BOARD
UNTIL I GOT INTO ANOTHER SCHOOL
ANOTHER SCHOOL
AND NOW I'M HERE

NO BLAIR
NO BUSH
NO QUEEN

THEY DIDN'T HELP TO WRITE ENGLISH BUT
BENIN
WELL I KNEW BENIN ALREADY
WASTING MY TIME DOING SOMETHING
I COULD HAVE DONE AT HOME
SHOULD HAVE BEEN LEARNING TO SPEAK
ENGLISH
LEARNING LIFE ABOUT HOW TO BE ENGLISH
BUT THEY HAD ME MAKING FAIRY CAKES

NO BLAIR
NO BUSH
NO QUEEN

Patience Emwanta aged 16

Printed in the United Kingdom
by Lightning Source UK Ltd.
129855UK00001B/442-483/P